POP CULTURE
REVOLUTIONS

GAMERS
UNITE!

THE VIDEO GAME REVOLUTION

by Shane Frederick

Content Adviser: Gary Geisler, Ph.D., Assistant Professor, School of Information,
University of Texas at Austin

Reading Adviser: Alexa L. Sandmann, Ed.D., Professor of Literacy, College and
Graduate School of Education, Health, and Human Services, Kent State University

COMPASS POINT BOOKS
a capstone imprint

Compass Point Books
151 Good Counsel Drive
Box 669
Mankato, MN 56002-0669

This book was manufactured with paper containing
at least 10 percent post-consumer waste.

Managing Editor: Catherine Neitge
Designer: Veronica Bianchini
Photo Researcher: Eric Gohl
Library Consultant: Kathleen Baxter
Production Specialist: Jane Klenk

Library of Congress Cataloging-in-Publication Data
Frederick, Shane.
  Gamers unite! : the video game revolution / by Shane Frederick.
      p. cm.—(Pop culture revolutions)
  Includes bibliographical references and index.
  ISBN 978-0-7565-4244-3 (library binding)
  1. Video games—History—Juvenile literature. I. Title. II. Series.
  GV1469.3.F74 2010
  794.809—dc22   2009030750

Visit Compass Point Books on the Internet at *www.compasspointbooks.com*
  or e-mail your request to *custserv@compasspointbooks.com*

TABLE OF CONTENTS

INTRODUCTION
Shall We Play a Game?

"What's so special about playing games with some machine?" Ally Sheedy's character in the 1983 film *WarGames*, Jennifer Mack, rolls her eyes when she asks that question. In the popular movie, computer nerd David Lightman (played by Matthew Broderick) accidentally hacks into the military system that launches nuclear missiles. He doesn't realize it. He's just trying to find the coolest new video games before they hit the market.

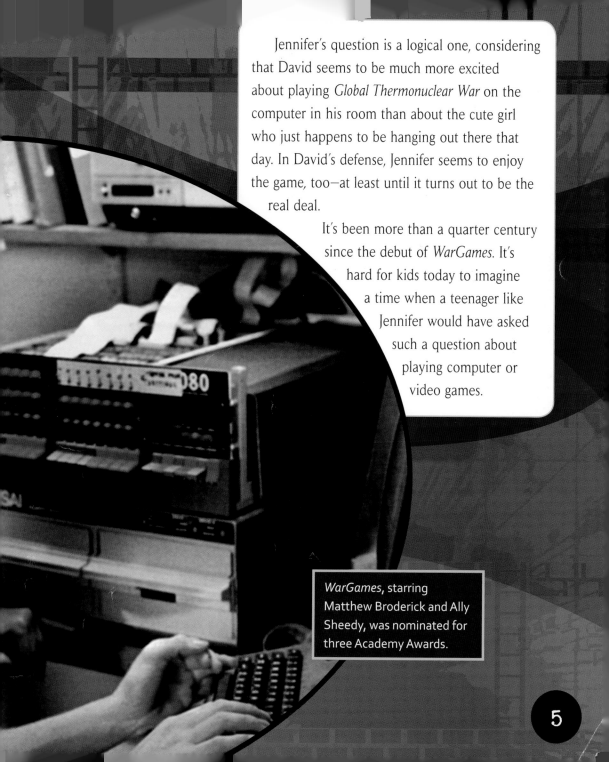

Jennifer's question is a logical one, considering that David seems to be much more excited about playing *Global Thermonuclear War* on the computer in his room than about the cute girl who just happens to be hanging out there that day. In David's defense, Jennifer seems to enjoy the game, too—at least until it turns out to be the real deal.

It's been more than a quarter century since the debut of *WarGames*. It's hard for kids today to imagine a time when a teenager like Jennifer would have asked such a question about playing computer or video games.

WarGames, starring Matthew Broderick and Ally Sheedy, was nominated for three Academy Awards.

According to a 2007–2008 study by the Pew Internet & American Life Project, a whopping 97 percent of young people ages 12 to 17—including 99 percent of boys and 94 percent of girls—play video games.

They play on their TVs, computers, and handheld devices. They play *Guitar Hero* with their friends, *World of Warcraft* with thousands of others online, and even *Wii Sports* with their parents.

And guess what—this pop culture revolution is still happening! Curious? Put down that Game Boy and turn the page. …

Best sellers

Video games have become a multibillion-dollar-a-year industry, surpassing movies. Here are the top-selling game series:

1. Super Mario Bros. (200 million units)
2. Pokémon (155 million)
3. The Sims (100 million)
4. Tetris (86 million)
5. Final Fantasy (80 million)
6. Grand Theft Auto (76 million)
7. Madden NFL (70 million)
8. FIFA soccer (65 million)
9. The Legend of Zelda (52 million)
10. Tom Clancy (50 million)

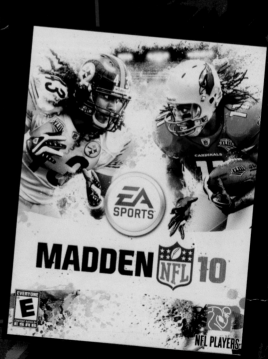

Two boys played the latest *Madden NFL* game during a tournament at the Dallas Cowboys' stadium in Texas.

CHAPTER 1
It's Revolutionary!

The video games are coming! The video games are coming! If anyone had listened to him, Ralph Baer might now be known as the Paul Revere of video games. But few heard him when he first made a revolutionary prediction almost 60 years ago.

Ralph Baer played ping-pong in 2006 on his Brown Box , which is on display at the Computerspiele Museum in Berlin, Germany.

Ralph Baer began his career as an electrical engineer in the 1940s. He designed television sets before TVs were a staple in every American home. Back then, Baer didn't see a nation of couch potatoes staring slack-jawed at the small screen. As early as 1951, he envisioned people interacting with their TVs. He thought people would like to play games on them.

Sounds like a no-brainer, right? Well, a lot of people told Baer it was a dumb idea. But 15 years and 60 million TV sets later, Baer hadn't forgotten his idea.

In the late 1960s, he finally began working on his device. He tested and tried to play ping-pong, golf, and shooting games on his TV. Most important, he secured a patent for his concept, making him the inventor of the home video game. The first shot of the revolution was fired—and the trigger was a button on Ralph Baer's Brown Box.

Among his box's games was a ping-pong game that Atari later turned into the country's first popular and commercially successful arcade and home game—*Pong*. By the mid-1970s, more and more video games began popping up in homes and arcades across the country and around the world.

Pong: It was big

The first video game to take the world by storm was *Pong*. It started bouncing back and forth on college campuses and in bars in 1972 and entered people's homes a short time later.

Pong wasn't the first arcade video game, though. A year earlier, *Computer Space* started gobbling up spare quarters. Like *Pong*, *Computer Space* was created by Atari founder Nolan Bushnell. It was based on what is believed to be the first fully interactive video game, *Spacewar!* That early game was created and played on a mainframe computer at the Massachusetts Institute of Technology in 1962 and later was put on computers at other college campuses. It was also the first in a long line of games to feature spaceships, laser beams, and aliens.

Super-simple video games were created even earlier. A tic-tac-toe game for TV sets called *Noughts and Crosses* was first played in 1952, and *Tennis for Two* made an appearance in 1958.

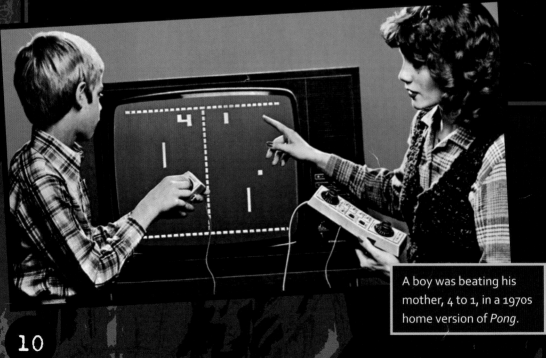

A boy was beating his mother, 4 to 1, in a 1970s home version of *Pong*.

The revolution started simply, with a lone dot bouncing back and forth across the screen. It has become a world of seemingly infinite concepts and storylines in which players now swing controllers like tennis rackets. Or they putt not *like* but *as* Tiger Woods and, of course, fire guns—lots of guns—in the roles of duck hunters and soldiers, car thieves, and mafia hit men.

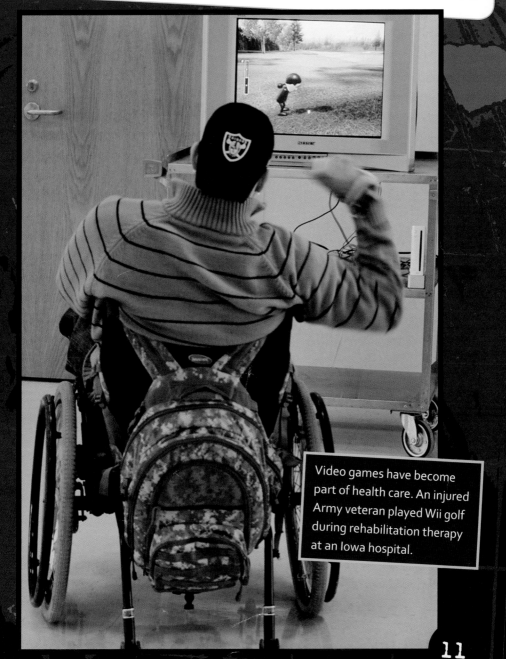

Video games have become part of health care. An injured Army veteran played Wii golf during rehabilitation therapy at an Iowa hospital.

In less than 40 years, video games have become a multibillion-dollar-a-year business, surpassing the movie and music industries, as hundreds of millions of people, young and old, play games every day.

Why did video games become so popular so fast? It seems that Ralph Baer's theory was right—people wanted to do more with their TVs than just watch shows.

Before the arrival of radio and television, people left home to find most of their entertainment. But radios and TV sets brought music, theater, and sports right into everyone's living room. Video games brought carnival games into the house.

A 2009 study by Nielsen Media Research, the company that studies who watches what on TV, discovered that video games had essentially become "the fifth TV network" along with ABC, CBS, NBC, and Fox. In other words, a TV is more likely to have a video game going on its screen than a show on the CW network.

More than 35 years ago, Baer's Brown Box led to the Magnavox Odyssey, the very first in-home video

Released in the late 1970s, the Odyssey 2001 was the European version of the popular Magnavox system. It played three games in color—tennis, hockey, and squash.

game system. It had no sound and games were in black and white. While that might not sound like much fun by today's high-definition, surround-sound standards, people clamored to play. In 1972 and 1973, after a slow start, 300,000 Odysseys were sold, and the console wars had begun.

SEY 2001

rills on your TV screen

ODYSSEY 2001

In the 1970s, game system sales took off. The Atari 2600 game console was the machine every kid wanted, and eventually 30 million homes had it. In the 1980s, it was the Nintendo Entertainment System, which came bundled with the extremely popular game *Super Mario Bros.* In the 1990s, the Sony PlayStation hauled in the cash, selling 2 million systems in the U.S. in its first year of existence. Its second version, PlayStation 2, sold nearly 140 million units by the time PS3 came along. In the mid-2000s, the bar continued to rise as computer giant Microsoft introduced the Xbox and Nintendo created the Wii. The Wii's accompanying sports package included a game that took *Pong* to a whole new level by transforming living rooms into tennis courts.

Satoru Iwata, who became president of Nintendo in 2002, is credited with much of the company's success.

Add to that list Nintendo Game Boys and other portable, handheld systems as well as home computers and the Internet, and it seems you can't swing a joystick around anywhere without bumping into some kid—or adult—sitting in front of a screen and playing a video game.

Forty years after Baer began testing his first game console, video games have even become educational tools. They're now being used in schools to help students learn everything from reading and writing to math and social studies.

The U.S. military uses interactive simulation games to train soldiers who are about to go on foreign missions on how to handle difficult situations.

Everybody wants one

Nintendo has sold nearly 120 million Game Boy handheld systems around the world plus another 80 million units of the Game Boy Advance system. In addition, 100 million Nintendo DS systems have been sold. It is the best-selling game system of all time.

Gym class revolution

Video games are often fingered as a culprit in the childhood obesity epidemic.

Certainly most gamers give little more than their thumbs a workout when they're plopped down in front of their TVs and PCs.

But rather than calling for a ban on games, some physical education teachers have embraced them, most notably *Dance Dance Revolution*.

Hundreds of schools in the United States use the game in gym classes, and the number is expected to climb to 1,500. Students start sweating and get their hearts pumping as they groove to the beat and follow arrows on the screen by boogying onto corresponding spots on the game's floor mat.

How popular is it? Said a longtime West Virginia gym teacher: "They don't run in here like that for basketball."

When President Barack Obama was running for office, he certainly knew the far reach of video games. In the weeks before the November 2008 election, his campaign bought advertising space in some Xbox 360 video games. The ads appeared on virtual billboards and other signs in games that download information from the Internet during play.

For years parents told their children that they were sitting too close to the TV and were hurting their eyes. But over the last four decades, lots of kids apparently haven't been listening—people everywhere were staring straight into screens.

Students in Fargo, North Dakota, move to *Dance Dance Revolution* during gym class.

CHAPTER 2

It's All in the Game

It was a scene that played out in cities all across America. The lines stretched out the door and down the block. Those at the front had been camped there for hours. Those at the back wondered whether they'd get what they came for once the clock struck midnight and the cash registers started ringing.

The excitement and anticipation weren't for tickets for a popular concert or the newest blockbuster movie. Those in line wanted to make sure they were among the first to buy and play the latest version of the football video game *Madden NFL 10*, an edition of one of the most successful video game series of all time.

Curse or coincidence?

Every year fans of the *Madden NFL* series eagerly anticipate the latest version of the game. Pro football players might fear it, though, because the game's cover boys haven't always had good luck.

Here are victims of the so-called Madden Curse—all of the players who have appeared on the game's last nine covers have run into trouble:

- 2002: Vikings quarterback Daunte Culpepper (knee injury)

- 2003: Rams running back Marshall Faulk (ankle injury)

- 2004: Falcons quarterback Michael Vick (broken leg; prison)

- 2005: Ravens linebacker Ray Lewis (broken arm)

- 2006: Eagles quarterback Donovan McNabb (hernia surgery)

- 2007: Seahawks running back Shaun Alexander (broken foot)

- 2008: Titans quarterback Vince Young (missed first game since middle school)

- 2009: Packers quarterback Brett Favre (retired, came out of retirement, traded to Jets)

- 2010: Steelers safety Troy Polamalu (knee injury)

Today video games share center stage of popular culture, along with movies, music, books, television shows, and sports. Gamers mark the days off on their calendars as they await the release of new versions of their favorite games, just as a fan of the Jonas Brothers might anticipate the rock band's latest CD. Newspapers and other publications review video games, just as they do books and movies.

It didn't take long for video games to seep into our everyday lives.

In the early 1970s, *Pong* drew crowds around its machines at arcades when it was first plugged in. Players tried to keep the "ball" (a white dot) moving back and forth by controlling a "paddle" (a white bar) that moved up and down. (You had to have a good imagination.)

Pong was the first of four arcade games to earn more than $1 billion. *Space Invaders, Pac-Man,* and *Defender* also took the world by storm in their day and hit that milestone, too. Of course, all of those games eventually became available in home versions for video game consoles and, by the early 1980s, on personal computers.

Home gamers, though, began looking for more than just copies of arcade games to play from their sofas and easy chairs. Young people especially soon realized that they had a lot more time to invest in a game than the three minutes it took for Blinky, Pinky, Inky, and Clyde to overtake Pac-Man down at the local pizzeria.

The popularity and earnings of arcade video games peaked in the early 1980s.

Shigeru Miyamoto, a Japanese video game designer, had new ideas. Miyamoto is famous for creating the arcade game *Donkey Kong* and inventing the character Mario. In Miyamoto's imaginative game, *Super Mario Bros.*, players took Mario or his brother, Luigi, on a mission through several worlds in the Mushroom Kingdom to save Princess Peach. During Mario's mission, he had to avoid evil mushrooms and turtles, as well as fireball-spitting flowers. He could stomp on the mushrooms, kick turtle shells, and collect coins to gain additional lives.

Shigeru Miyamoto started his career with Nintendo as an artist.

Mario's the man

Everybody's favorite little Italian plumber, Mario, may be the most popular character in video game history. Originally called Jumpman, Mario (often with his brother, Luigi) has appeared in more than 200 video games since first trying to save the damsel in distress, Pauline, in *Donkey Kong* in 1981.

Some of the games Mario has starred in:

- *Super Mario Bros.*
- *Dr. Mario*
- *Super Mario World*
- *Mario Teaches Typing*
- *Mario vs. Donkey Kong*
- *Mario Kart*
- *Mario Tennis*
- *Mario Golf*
- *Super Smash Bros.*
- *Mario & Sonic at the Olympic Games*

Suddenly players had a whole new world to explore while they played. They weren't just moving a character from point A to point B to complete a level. Miyamoto said he wanted to make the players themselves "the stars of the game," and his games put them smack dab in the middle of the story.

It's hard to believe that anything could have stopped the momentum of the video game revolution. But between 1982 and 1984, the industry was in shambles. The market was becoming saturated with games and gaming systems, and many were just no fun to play. Gaming companies lost massive amounts of money, and some even went bankrupt.

And then came Miyamoto and *Super Mario Bros.* to revive the dying industry. Miyamoto hit the jackpot again with the creation of the fantasy-adventure game *The Legend of Zelda* in 1986.

Dead and buried

In 1982 Atari probably thought it had a slam-dunk best-selling video game based on the hit movie *E.T.: The ExtraTerrestrial.* But it was a flop and is still considered by many to be one of the worst video games of all time. Critics called it poorly designed, dull, and repetitive.

If you're looking for a copy of the game, grab your shovel, because 14 truckloads of unwanted *E.T.* game cartridges were dumped into a landfill in New Mexico and buried under a slab of concrete.

Like *Donkey Kong* and *Super Mario Bros.*, *Zelda* was another rescue-the-princess game, but this one had even more to see. As the hero, Link, sought Princess Zelda, he had to solve puzzles, fight battles, race other characters, and explore the land to advance through the levels.

It changed the way people played video games. For one thing, *Zelda* introduced role-playing games to the mainstream. But it also included a battery pack that allowed players to save their progress. That let them pick up where they left off in *Zelda's* long story. It was like using a bookmark to keep the reader's place in a novel. The influence of *The Legend of Zelda* can be seen in some of today's most popular games.

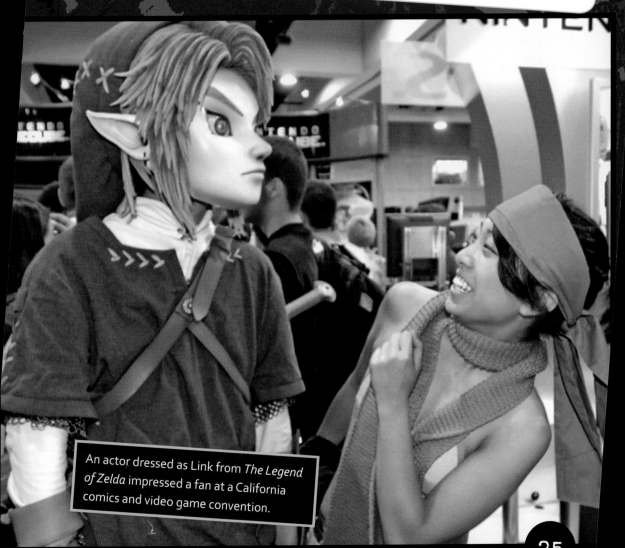

An actor dressed as Link from *The Legend of Zelda* impressed a fan at a California comics and video game convention.

In 1993 the game *Myst* was released, and it became a surprise hit. For nearly 10 years it was the best-selling computer game of all time. Players weren't told much about how to play or how to win. They had to just start exploring a mysterious deserted island. Players had to solve puzzles and find and follow clues along the way. The game had various endings depending on how it was played.

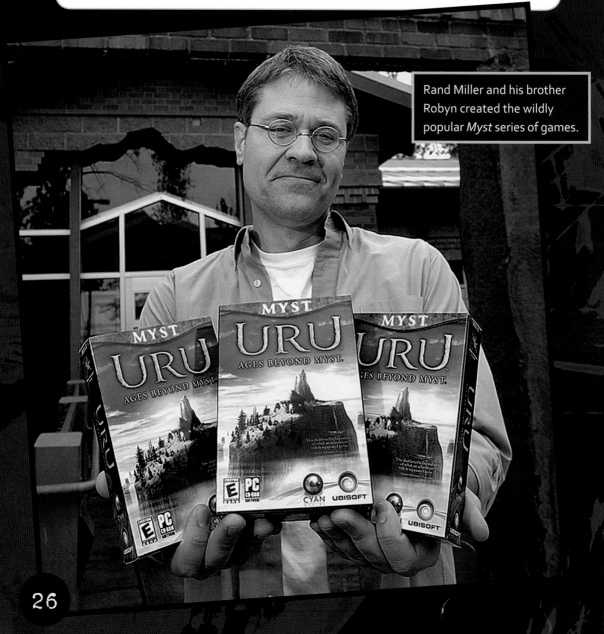

Rand Miller and his brother Robyn created the wildly popular *Myst* series of games.

In *Grand Theft Auto III*, which was released in 2001, players got almost complete freedom to explore and do whatever they wanted in the game. That included some violent and other highly questionable, if not immoral, actions, even if they were well outside the game's plot.

Still other games did not have a plot or an endgame.

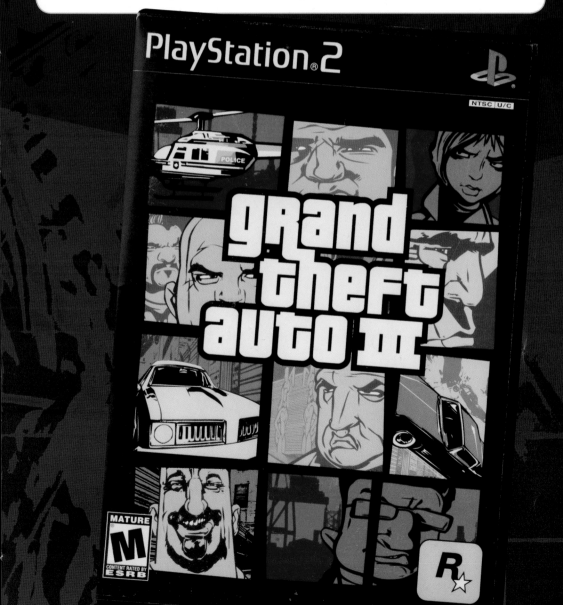

Meet *The Sims*

Strange as it may seem, the best-selling computer game in history isn't a shoot-'em-up game or a sports game or even a fantasy-world game.

It's *The Sims*, a life-simulation game in which players control the ordinary, everyday lives of ordinary, everyday people in an ordinary, everyday neighborhood.

Released in 2000, the original game sold 16 million copies worldwide. And that was before the release of several sequels and expansion packs, such as *The Sims House Party*, *The Sims Vacation*, and *The Sims Hot Date*. You can even play the latest *Sims* game on your iPhone!

The object of all the games is to make choices for the simulated people, such as deciding how they will spend their money and where they will live.

They even have to make sure their characters eat and go to the bathroom. If they don't, well, it's pretty realistic, so you can probably guess what happens next.

Games such as *Civilization* and *The Sims* allowed players full control—good and bad—over the game's world and its inhabitants' lives. In 2008 *Spore* gave players a chance to create their own evolving creatures and universes, starting only with single-cell organisms.

Players love these games. They get to be masters of their worlds.

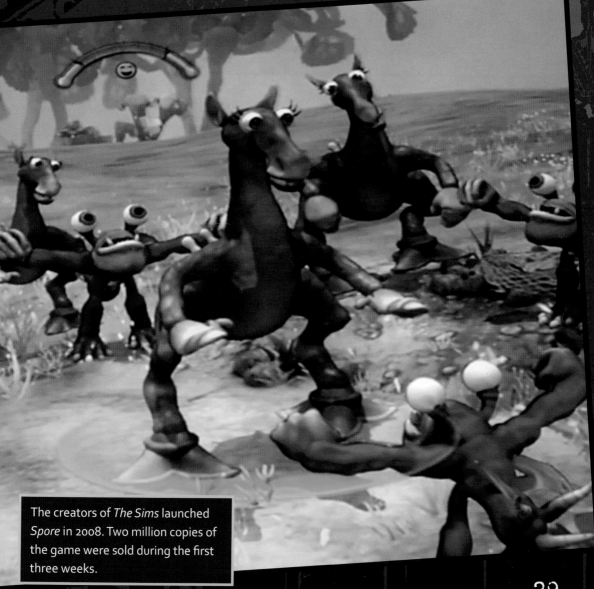

The creators of *The Sims* launched *Spore* in 2008. Two million copies of the game were sold during the first three weeks.

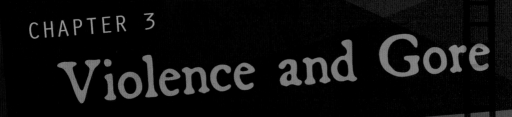

CHAPTER 3

Violence and Gore

Like many revolutions, the video game revolution has come with guns and violence. Some of the first video games, after all, were shooting games.

The arcade game *Computer Space* was released in 1971, the year before *Pong*. It took place in outer space with starships and flying saucers firing laser beams at each other. Things were getting blown up, and gamers loved it. Later, car-racing games often ended in fiery crashes.

Then there was that oafish gorilla, Donkey Kong, who was trying to knock off Mario by tossing barrels at him, trying to send him to his death. *Dance Dance Revolution* it was not.

Donkey Kong first appeared in 1981 and has been chasing Mario ever since.

Controversial from the start

The controversy about video game violence is almost as old as the games themselves.

One of the first games to shock parents and other adults was the 1976 arcade game *Death Race*, which was based on the 1975 cult hit movie *Death Race 2000*, starring Sylvester Stallone and David Carradine.

The object of the game was the same as the theme of the movie, which had the tagline "In the year 2000 hit and run driving is no longer a crime. It's the national sport!"

In the game, cross-country car racers score points by running down pedestrians. Whenever a person is hit, there is a screaming sound and the person is replaced by a cross-shaped tombstone.

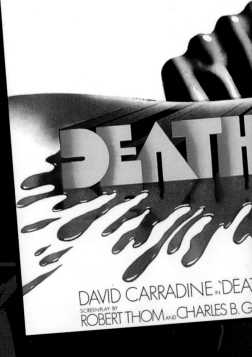

In the year 2000 hit and run driving is no longer a crime. It's the NATIONAL SPORT !

DEATH

DAVID CARRADINE in DEA
SCREENPLAY BY
ROBERT THOM AND CHARLES B. G

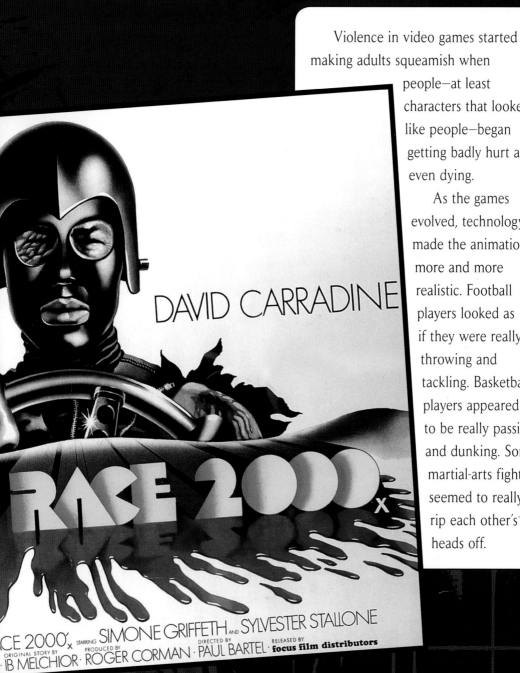

Violence in video games started making adults squeamish when people—at least characters that looked like people—began getting badly hurt and even dying.

As the games evolved, technology made the animation more and more realistic. Football players looked as if they were really throwing and tackling. Basketball players appeared to be really passing and dunking. Some martial-arts fighters seemed to really rip each other's heads off.

Mortal Kombat, with its excessive violence and gore, was particularly shocking. It first hit the arcades in 1992 and was on Sega home systems shortly after. The characters were photographic depictions of actors who posed for the game designers to show realistic kicking and punching. At the end of a fight, the winner got to finish off the loser, often in a blood-soaked decapitation. This competitive killing game was extremely popular. It was the best-selling game of 1993.

The U.S. Congress took notice of *Mortal Kombat* and other violent games of the era and called for hearings. Joseph Lieberman, a U.S. senator from Connecticut, was especially appalled, saying, "These games are no mark of a civilized society."

Mortal Kombat has inspired TV shows, movies, and graphic novels.

Lieberman demanded that the video game industry come up with a rating system, which it did. He and a U.S. senator from Wisconsin, Herb Kohl, created an annual report card on video games for families. The issue is still often debated in Washington.

Illinois tried to pass a law banning the sale of violent video games to minors. But the law was struck down by a federal judge who said it violated the right to free speech guaranteed by the First Amendment to the Constitution.

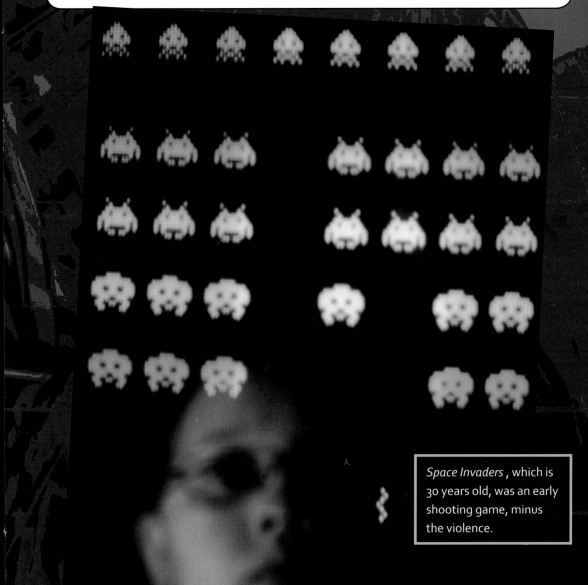

Space Invaders, which is 30 years old, was an early shooting game, minus the violence.

OK TO PLAY?

CHECK THE RATINGS *ON EVERY* VIDEO GAME BOX.

To take full advantage of the ESRB Rating System, it is important for parents and other customers to check the Rating Symbol suggesting age appropriateness on the front of the game package, and the content descriptor on the back of the package. Content descriptors indicate elements in a game that may have triggered a particular rating and may be of interest or concern.

ON FRONT OF GAME PACKAGING

Early Childhood	May be suitable for ages 3 and older. Contains no material that parents would find inappropriate.
Everyone	May be suitable for ages 6 and older. Titles in this category may contain minimal cartoon, fantasy or mild violence and/or use of mild language.
Everyone 10+	May be suitable for ages 10 and older. Titles in this category may contain more cartoon, fantasy or mild violence, mild language, and/or minimal suggestive themes.
Teen	May be suitable for ages 13 and older. Titles in this category may contain violence, suggestive themes, crude humor, minimal blood, simulated gambling, and/or infrequent use of strong language.
Mature	May be suitable for ages 17 and older. Titles in this category may contain intense violence, blood and gore, sexual content, and/or strong language.
Adults Only	Should only be played by persons 18 years and older. Titles in this category may include prolonged scenes of intense violence and/or graphic sexual content and nudity.

ON BACK OF GAME PACKAGING

Content descriptors are found on the back of the box.
Go to www.ESRB.org for a complete listing of content descriptors.

www.ESRB.org

Ratings systems, report cards, and new laws didn't stop the violence. In some cases, it got more graphic and more realistic. In later games in the *Grand Theft Auto* series, a player could commit random acts of violence, including beating someone with a baseball bat, rather than follow the game's storyline.

Another type of game that causes concern is the first-person shooter game, in which a player sees the game through the eyes of a character who uses a weapon.

With realistic 3-D graphics, games such as *Doom, Quake*, and *Halo* allowed gamers to play as if they were right in the action. The only parts of the player that can be seen are hands, which are usually gripping and shooting a gun.

Researchers have argued for and against the notion that video game violence causes aggressive behavior and desensitizes gamers to real-life violence.

Immediately after the shootings at Columbine High School in Colorado, Virginia Tech University, and Northern Illinois University, some were quick to blame violent, first-person shooter games, including *Doom* and *Counter-Strike*, for the killers' behavior. But much of that criticism was thrown out the window when the killers' lives were studied. The Virginia Tech shooter, for instance, was not much of a gamer.

On the other hand, one researcher said a game like *Halo*, which is a multiplayer online role-playing game, also gives players opportunities to work together and help each other. Studies also have found that overall youth violence has decreased as video games have grown in popularity.

Fans stood in line for hours to buy *Halo 2* when it went on sale at midnight.

Others have insisted that it's the same violence-in-the-media controversy that's been debated for years, starting with books and later focusing on comics, movies, television, and rock music. Violent video games are only one slice of the pop culture pie. Of the top 10 best-selling video game series of all time, only one—*Grand Theft Auto*—is also a staple on lists of the 10 most violent video games.

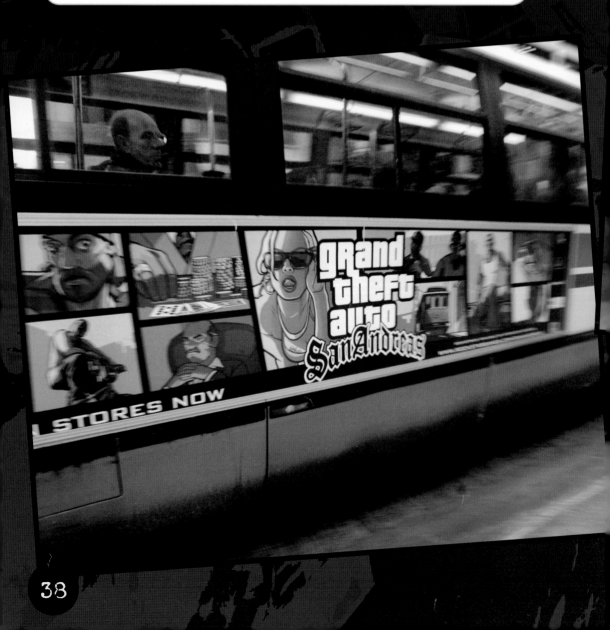

Sega Dreamcast featured many types of games, but its most popular was the nonviolent *Sonic Adventure*.

Yet there have been successful video games without realistic violence. A popular adventure series in the early 2000s was the Lego games series, which was based on such movies as those in the *Star Wars*, *Indiana Jones*, and *Batman* series of films. Instead of depicting real-life scenes and action, including some violence, the games have characters and sets that are made of the popular interlocking building blocks. No blood and guts are involved, just pieces that can come apart in fights and need to be picked up and put back together.

CHAPTER 4
Movin' and Groovin'

Late in 2006, during the holiday gift-buying season, people started to make way for the Wii. Literally.

Nintendo's new gaming console forced people to push furniture around and open up their TV rooms to make space to play the system's games. It came with controllers that needed more than just thumbs. People swung their remote controls like tennis rackets, golf clubs, and baseball bats while playing the *Wii Sports* game that was included with the console.

They threw punches and rolled bowling balls with them, too. Their actions translated to the avatars on the screens in front of them.

Players were so enthusiastic that Nintendo had to strengthen the wrist strap on the controller so it wouldn't fly off and cause body bruises, broken vases, and, worst of all, shattered television screens.

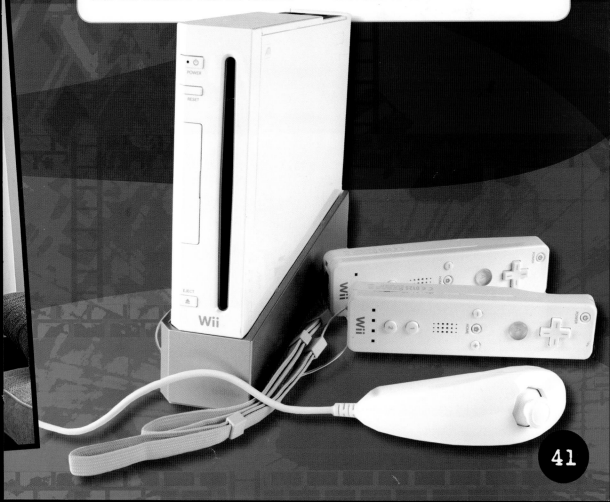

The Wii is popular with all ages. A Michigan senior center even hosts a Wii bowling league.

Still, the system drew almost universal praise for getting gamers, as well as a lot of nongamers, off the couch and on their feet. People got their blood pumping and started sweating to tennis and boxing games that were a far cry from *Pong* and *Punchout!!*

Makers of other games had to adapt them for the popular Wii, and they did. New games in the *Madden NFL* series let gamers play quarterback by making throwing motions with their remotes, receiver by putting their hands in the air, and linebacker by making tackling motions. The only thing more realistic was going out in the yard and playing a game of two-hand touch.

Sports games have long had crossover appeal. They attract non-geeks and older players to video gaming, something they might otherwise have scoffed at or ignored. The extremely popular *Madden NFL* series has been around since 1988.

The National Basketball Association, the National Hockey League, Major League Baseball, the Professional Golfers Association, and FIFA, the international governing body of soccer, have linked their products, teams, and players to popular video games.

More than 15 years after its release, the hockey game *NHL '94* is still considered by many to be the greatest sports video game of all time. In 2008 the basketball game *NBA Live 09* allowed players to connect to the Internet and download real-life statistics, trends, injuries, and other up-to-date information about their favorite players to increase realism.

Get in the game

Celebrities have lent their likenesses and voices to video games for years. Pro hockey and basketball players appear in the NHL and NBA series, and rock stars have given concerts in *The Sims* and battled *Guitar Hero* players. A few have gotten their names in the titles.

Some stars who have their own video games or game series:

- Tiger Woods (golfer)
- The Beatles (rock band)
- Tony Hawk (skateboarder)
- Aerosmith (rock band)
- 50 Cent (hip-hop artist)
- John Madden (football TV analyst)
- Mike Tyson (boxer)
- Mia Hamm (soccer player)
- Michelle Kwan (figure skater)
- Britney Spears (pop singer)
- Tom Clancy (author of spy novels)

While some true video game geeks aren't happy that the industry is trying to appeal more to mainstream audiences, there is simply no stopping game makers from expanding their market to include everybody, even parents. By 2009 Wii was the most popular video game format for adults, and, according to Nielsen, women over 35 years old—a lot of moms—made up one-third of adult players. Although these first-generation gamers felt old as they watched their children master high-tech games, many parents today are standing by their sides and playing right along.

Nintendo didn't just take on other gaming systems and media with the Wii. It took on health clubs and exercise TV shows when it introduced *Wii Fit*. Designed by Shigeru Miyamoto, *Wii Fit* let players play balance games and do yoga, strength training, and aerobics while standing on a balance board. They can save data indicating their daily progress.

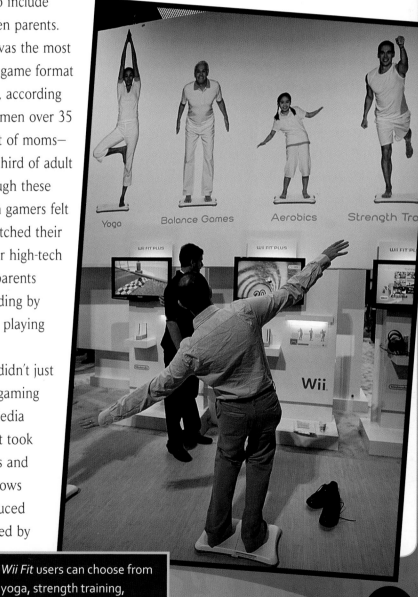

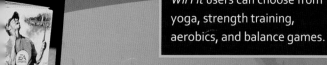
Wii Fit users can choose from yoga, strength training, aerobics, and balance games.

Music games have also attracted casual gamers. *Wii Music* allowed gamers to "play" a variety of musical instruments with the controllers. *Guitar Hero* and *Rock Band* became instant smash hits, capitalizing on the popularity of karaoke and people's fondness for playing air guitar in front of their bedroom mirrors.

Guitar Hero and *Rock Band* let gamers "play" their favorite songs. Instead of regular gamepads, the games came with controllers shaped like guitars and drum kits. *Guitar Hero* was packaged with guitars designed to look like famous six-string guitars made by Gibson.

The games became very popular at parties—nobody plays charades anymore—and bars and restaurants started to have *Guitar Hero* contests rather than live music to draw customers.

Pac-Man fever

Long before players started jamming on *Guitar Hero*, the video game industry had its first real rock star. He was a dot-chomping, ghost-chasing yellow blob named Pac-Man.

Pac-Man was introduced in American arcades in 1980 and quickly became one of the most popular games the medium has ever seen. It's been estimated that *Pac-Man* was played more than 10 billion times in the 20th century. That's billion, with a B.

Besides inspiring spin-off games such as the popular Ms. Pac-Man and several home versions, Pac-Man could be found in Saturday morning cartoons, on bed sheets, lunch boxes, and other memorabilia, and even on the radio.

In 1982 the song "Pac-Man Fever" by the one-hit wonder Buckner & Garcia became a top-10 hit.

The song's chorus went:

I got Pac-Man Fever
It's driving me crazy
I got Pac-Man Fever
I'm going out of my mind

Although the games used actual rock songs, a couple of bands, Aerosmith and Metallica, were given their own versions of *Guitar Hero,* using their songs and others that inspired their music. *Rock Band* went back to the 1960s with a version devoted to the music of one of the greatest rock bands of all time, The Beatles. The rockers' involvement in the game was another step in the melding of video games with other media. Video games had long been connected with movies and books.

When Metallica released *Death Magnetic* in 2008, it immediately made the album's songs available for downloading to play on *Guitar Hero III.* Some music critics complained that the sound was better in the video game than on the CD.

"It's cool for us to be pioneers helping to rebuild the music industry through a format like video games," Aerosmith guitarist Joe Perry said. "It's great for rock, since the record companies are struggling to make sense of how things are changing. Fans want to get and experience music in new formats—and there are going to be some of them who will play the game, then pick up the guitar for real and start bands. It's what's happening now, and it's only going to build more momentum in the future. It's a massive change for the music business."

Just a few years into the 21st century, the world of video games truly seemed to have something for everyone.

Metallica performed live to celebrate the release of the version of *Guitar Hero* that bears their name.

CHAPTER 5
A Different World

When the first video game was created, not only were computer geeks the first ones to play it, they were the only ones who could play it.

Spacewar!, the game that inspired the first coin-operated arcade game, *Computer Space,* was installed on mainframe computers at colleges across the country in the early 1960s. This was decades before nearly every college student had a laptop nearby during all waking hours. Back then computers were much, much bigger—some filled entire rooms—and access to them was limited.

Today nearly three-fourths of all homes in the United States have at least one computer, whether it's to surf the Web, balance family budgets, or download music and movies.

Oh yeah, a lot of people use them to play games.

A student worked on a computer at the Massachusetts Institute of Technology in 1966.

Consoles such as the Atari 2600 were, in fact, the first computers to enter homes. Today, even with the popularity of the Wii, the PlayStation, and the Xbox, regular personal computers are just as important to the gaming world. Whether you're looking online for free versions of classic games such as *Space Invaders*, playing *Mob Wars* or *Word Challenge* on Facebook, or plugging your Guitar Hero Gibson X-plorer into your Mac to try to master "Welcome to the Jungle," you are rockin' out on your computer.

Addicted to games?

How much is too much? Can gamers actually become addicted to video games? The possibility is being studied.

Certainly there are examples of obsessive game-playing behavior, such as people's playing for 24 hours straight, or spending an entire weekend alone in Azeroth—the land of *World of Warcraft*—and isolated from live social contact.

Some say that such behavior isn't much different from drug and alcohol abuse or compulsive gambling.

The problem some players have, especially those involved in massively multiplayer online role-playing games, is that they often see their avatars as themselves. They feel that they are too important to the game, especially to other players relying on them, to stop playing.

Army training, sir!

If almost every young person in the country is playing video games, could there be a better medium to use as a recruiting tool? The U.S. military sees its potential.

In 2002, a year before the war in Iraq began, the U.S. Army created the Web-based role-playing game *America's Army*, which could be downloaded for free from the Army's Web site. The game, whose players go through virtual basic training, weapons instruction, and combat, became one of the most popular action games in the country. By 2009 *America's Army* had nearly 10 million registered users.

THE OFFICIAL U.S. ARMY GAME

AMERICA'S ★ ARMY

EMPOWER YOURSEL

Dance Dance Revolution drew crowds at video arcades.

The computer boom has connected the entire planet online, so it's only natural that people have found a way to play games together in cyberspace.

Old-fashioned arcades and video game-based restaurants, including those in such national chains as GameWorks and Dave & Buster's, brought people together physically to play and to socialize, as did the Friday-night sleepover. Yet in terms of participation, those are nothing compared with what online games have done.

In 2009 more than 11.5 million people around the world were registered *World of Warcraft* players. By far the most popular of the massively multiplayer online role-playing games, *World of Warcraft* takes players—for a monthly fee—to a different world. There each player assumes the role of a hero, perhaps as a dwarf, gnome, or elf, on an adventure, along with thousands of other players. They go on quests where they can explore and earn experience and money to buy more weapons and skills. They can form alliances with other players. Along the way, they fight battles with dragons, orcs, or one another. The game never ends.

World of Warcraft and similar games, such as *Ultima Online* and *Star Wars Galaxies,* have disproved the notion that gamers are geeks playing alone in their basement bedrooms or nerds who only encounter each other at the computer lab. These games have shown that video games can have a social aspect that rivals that of other media, including TV, music, and movies.

Some *World of Warcraft* enthusiasts who met while playing online have even gotten married in virtual weddings attended online by fellow players. When players have died, friends in the form of their avatars have honored their lives online.

With people living in the virtual worlds of their favorite video games, the real world has had to adapt, just as it had to adapt to the rise of television and popular music.

Visitors at a games convention tested the newest version of *World of Warcraft*.

Video games on TV?

Even when the game console is turned off, you still can find games on TV.

In 2002 the TV network G4, created just for gamers, was launched. The network reaches 64 million homes through cable and satellite. It originally had shows devoted to various gaming genres, including action/adventure, sports, and multiplayer online role-playing games. One show even had its hosts hitting the road in search of the coolest new games.

As popular as video games have become, however, the network has never drawn the huge audience its creators hoped for. "These guys are online, not in front of the set like they used to be," a G4 executive said.

The network hasn't gone away, though, and its popular *Attack of the Show!* still covers the latest gaming news. G4 is trying to increase its audience by airing many nongaming programs, including *Ninja Warrior*, a Japanese obstacle course reality show.

Blair Butler of G4 interviewed a costumed guest at a comics and video game convention.

55

On the big screen

Several video games are based on movies. But there have been movies inspired by video games, too. Even *Asteroids*, more than 30 years after the game's original release, is headed for the big screen.

Other video games that have inspired movies:

- *Super Mario Bros.*
- *Mortal Kombat*
- *Pokémon*
- *Street Fighter*
- *Wing Commander*
- *Tomb Raider*
- *Final Fantasy*
- *Resident Evil*
- *Doom*
- *Max Payne*

Angelina Jolie starred as Lara Croft in *Tomb Raider.*

With hundreds of millions of dollars being spent to create games, they are now heavily advertised on TV and made into movies in order to find more people to buy and play them.

At the same time, with so many people playing video games every day, advertisers are finding ways to pitch their products in games. They believe they can reach more people this way than by just airing a commercial during a TV show.

Those trying to look into the future envision musicians releasing songs exclusively to players of popular games and holding virtual events in which gamers are asked to "show up" at a certain place at a certain time in their not-so-little online world. Some see a day when an awards show for video games rivals the Oscars and Emmys shows in interest and importance.

Video games are a hit at nursing homes.

Video games have been around long enough that a second generation of players—and in some cases, a third—is growing up with them, so it should not be surprising that so many people are playing them every day.

There are games for old and young, boys and girls, sports fans and thrill seekers, adventurers and puzzle solvers.

There are games that take three minutes, others that take three hours, and still others that never end. There are games that teach and others that are simply for fun.

What's so special about playing games with some machine?

It's what we do now.

Timeline

1962 ·············· *Spacewar!* is written on a mainframe computer at the Massachusetts Institute of Technology

1966 ·············· Ralph Baer begins work on a TV video game that he hopes to patent

1971 ·············· *Computer Space* becomes the first coin-operated arcade video game

1972 ·············· *Pong* first appears in arcades; Magnavox's Odyssey becomes the first home gaming system

1974 ·············· *TV Basketball* becomes the first game to use human figures

1976 ·············· *Night Driver* is the first game with a game player's perspective; *Breakout,* a popular game similar to *Pong,* is introduced

1977 ·············· Atari releases the Atari 2600 home console

1978 ·············· *Space Invaders* attacks for the first time

1980 ·············· *Pac-Man* starts gobbling dots—and quarters—in North America

1981 ·············· *Donkey Kong* barrels onto the scene

1983 ·············· Video game sales drop significantly

1985 ·············· The industry bounces back with the release of the Nintendo Entertainment System; *Super Mario Bros.* and *Tetris* are released

1986 ·············· *The Legend of Zelda* is first told

1989 ·············· Nintendo makes games portable with the Game Boy; Sega introduces its Genesis console

1990 ·············· *SimCity* comes to life

1991 ·············· *Sonic the Hedgehog* starts rolling and eventually becomes Sega's mascot

1992 •••••••••• *Mortal Kombat* starts throwing down in arcades; the first 3-D games, such as *Virtual Racing* and *Wolfenstein 3-D,* are released

1993 •••••••••• *Myst* lands for the first time; *Doom* is introduced; the U.S. Senate has hearings on video game violence

1994 •••••••••• A ratings system for video games is established

1995 •••••••••• Sony joins the revolution with its PlayStation

1996 •••••••••• Digipen Institute of Technology becomes the first college to offer a degree in video game development

1997 •••••••••• Ultima Online popularizes massively multiplayer online role-playing games

1998 •••••••••• *Dance Dance Revolution* and *Grand Theft Auto* are released

2000 •••••••••• *The Sims* shows up in the neighborhood; in three years it becomes the best-selling home computer game of all time

2001 •••••••••• Computer giant Microsoft joins the revolution with its Xbox

2002 •••••••••• G4, the first TV network devoted to the world of gaming, is launched

2005 •••••••••• *Guitar Hero* plays its first concert

2006 •••••••••• Nintendo gets people moving with the Wii

2009 •••••••••• More than 11.5 million people worldwide are online playing *World of Warcraft*

Glossary

animation | creating the appearance of moving images with drawings or computer graphics

arcade | business with an area where video games and other games are played

avatar | character or icon that represents a certain person in a video game

Bill of Rights | first 10 amendments to the U.S. Constitution

bundle | to package together; some games are bundled for sale with a game system

console | device that connects to a television for video game playing

endgame | final stage of a game

engineer | designer or builder of machines or other things

hack | to break into a computer system without permission

mainframe | large, high-speed computer

patent | right to be the only one to make, use, or sell an invention for a certain number of years

release date | when something, such as a video game, first becomes available to the public

saturated | to become soaked or full

simulation | computer model of how something could be in real life

Additional Resources

Ashcraft, Brian. *Arcade Mania!: The Turbo-Charged World of Japan's Game Centers*. New York: Kodansha International, 2008.

Berens, Kate, and Geoff Howard. *The Rough Guide to Videogames*. New York: Rough Guides, 2008.

Bruce, Linda, Sam Bruce, and Jack Bruce. *Entertainment Technology*. North Mankato, Minn.: Smart Apple Media, 2006.

DeMaria, Rusel, and Johnny L. Wilson. *High Score! The Illustrated History of Electronic Games*. New York: McGraw-Hill/Osborne, 2004.

Haugen, David M., ed. *Video Games*. Detroit: Greenhaven Press/Thomson Gale, 2008.

Katz, Jon. *Geeks: How Two Lost Boys Rode the Internet Out of Idaho*. New York: Villard Books, 2000.

Woodford, Chris, and Jon Woodcock. *Cool Stuff 2.0 and How It Works*. New York: DK Publishing, 2007.

FactHound

FactHound offers a safe, fun way to find Internet sites related to this book. All of the sites on FactHound have been researched by our staff.

Here's all you do:
Visit *www.facthound.com*
FactHound will fetch the best sites for you!

Select Bibliography

Baer, Ralph H. *Videogames: In the Beginning.* Springfield, N.J.: Rolenta Press, 2005.

Bellis, Mary. "Computer and Video Game History." About.com: Inventors. 21 July 2009. http://inventors.about.com/library/inventors/blcomputer_videogames.htm

Benedetti, Winda. "Playing the blame game: Why search our souls when video games make such an easy scapegoat?" MSNBC. 18 Feb. 2008. 21 July 2009. www.msnbc.msn.com/id/23204875/

Croal, N'Gai. "You Don't Have to Be a Nerd." *Newsweek.* 9 Aug. 2008. 11 Nov. 2009. www.newsweek.com/id/151759

Irvine, Martha. "Survey: Nearly every American kid plays video games." *USA Today.* 16 Sept. 2008. 11 Nov. 2009. www.usatoday.com/tech/gaming/2008-09-16-american-kids-gamers_N.htm

Kalning, Kristin. "If next-gen games are now, then what's next?" MSNBC. 25 Feb. 2008. 21 July 2009. www.msnbc.msn.com/id/23257066/

Kent, Steven L. *The Ultimate History of Video Games: From Pong to Pokémon and Beyond: The Story Behind the Craze That Touched Our Lives and Changed the World.* Roseville, Calif.: Prima Publishing, 2001.

Levin, Gary. "G4 network tries a new game plan to get more guys." *USA Today.* 24 March 2008. 21 July 2009. www.usatoday.com/tech/gaming/2008-03-24-G4-network_N.htm

Select Bibliography

Loguidice, Bill, and Matt Barton. *Vintage Games: An Insider Look at the History of Grand Theft Auto, Super Mario, and the Most Influential Games of All Time.* Boston: Focal Press/Elsevier, 2009.

Noer, Michael. "The Future of Videogames." Forbes.com. 11 Feb. 2008. 21 July 2009. www.forbes.com/2008/02/08/future-video-games-tech-future07-cx_mn_de_0211game.html

Peckham, Matt. "Yes We Can, Says Obama, in Video Games Everywhere." *PC World.* 15 Oct. 2008. 21 July 2009. www.pcworld.com/article/152323/yes_we_can_says_obama_in_video_games_everywhere.html

Pham, Alex. "Marathon sessions take over players: Is that sick?" *Los Angeles Times.* 22 June 2007. 21 July 2009. http://articles.latimes.com/2007/jun/22/business/fi-addict22

Schiesel, Seth. "P.E. Classes Turn to Video Game That Works Legs." *The New York Times.* 30 April 2007. 21 July 2009. www.nytimes.com/2007/04/30/health/30exer.html

Shields, Mike. "Nielsen: Video Games Approach 5th Network Status." *Adweek.* 25 March 2009. 21 July 2009. www.adweek.com/aw/content_display/news/agency/e3i4f087b1aeac6f008d0ecadfeffe4a191

The Video Game Revolution. PBS. 2004. 24 July 2009. www.pbs.org/kcts/videogamerevolution

Wolf, Mark J.P., ed. *The Medium of the Video Game.* Austin: University of Texas Press, 2002.

Wolf, Mark J.P., ed. *The Video Game Explosion: A History from PONG to Playstation and Beyond.* Westport, Conn.: Greenwood Press, 2008.

Look for the other books in this series:

YOU CAN'T READ THIS!
Why Books Get Banned

PLAY IT LOUD!
The Rebellious History of Music

GRAPHIC CONTENT!
The Culture of Comic Books

Index

About the Author

Shane Frederick is a sportswriter who lives in
Mankato, Minnesota, with his wife, Sara, their three
children, Ben, Jack, and Lucy, and their dog, Molly.
He covers college hockey and recreational sports
for *The Free Press.* He enjoys music, drawing, tennis,
and curling. And video games, of course.